Encountering
Christlikeness

Julia,

May you continue
to grow in the
likeness of Christ

[signature]

Encountering Christlikeness

Devotional Portraits of Christ-Like Behavior

———~———

Brad Simon

Published by:

Christian Growth Ministry

Encountering Christlikeness

Dedication

This book is dedicated to Debbie Simon, my best friend, my sweetheart, and my wife. She has provided me with loving support throughout my adult life and has been a valuable asset in my teaching ministry.

A Special Thanks to all the members of the Enrich Cafe critic group lead by Beebe and Katy Kauffman. Their encouragement, advice, and correction have helped me refine my style of writing and made me a better writer.

A Gift for You

Do you find it hard to put your thoughts into your prayers?

When you don't know what to pray, it can feel like your prayers are falling on deaf ears. That's where the Daily Prayer Guide & Journal comes in. With this guide, you'll always have a place to start your prayers.

In appreciation for your time reading this book, we would like to offer you a bonus gift — our new Daily Prayer Guide & Journal.

This Daily Prayer Guide & Journal is a simple, practical, and convenient way to help you stay consistent with your prayers. The printable guide & journal provides space for listing your personal prayer needs and topical prompts for your daily prayers.

To download your Free Daily Prayer Guide and Journal, go to: ChristianGrowthMinistry.com/guide

**Daily Prayer
Guide and Journal**

Get The Ebook

Table of Contents

Introduction

Grab a cup of coffee or favorite beverage and close the door to your room. Sit down, relax, and let your imagination take you back in time, on an exciting journey through the Gospels. In these short easy-to-read narratives, you will encounter various people who exemplified godly characteristics. Some we know their names, others are nameless faces in the crowd, but all provide powerful examples of Christ-like characteristics that made a welcome difference in the lives of people around them.

As you read these devotions, I encourage you to prayerfully consider specific actions God is leading you to take. The application of scripture in our life is our ultimate goal. Following each devotion, space is provided called Action Steps, for you to personalize the message. May your responses become a record filled with many discoveries and commitments along your magnificent journey in the Christian life.

My sincere desire and fervent prayer is that through these narratives, you will experience the emotions and passions of the people involved in these Biblical accounts. Most importantly, these narratives will inspire and motivate you to reflect Christ in your life, and deepen your understanding and appreciation of the Bible.

Discover how you can grow in the image of Christ. I present *Encountering Christlikeness*.

Brad Simon

The Little Lunch that Changed Everything

Matthew 14:13-21; Mark 6:30-44; Luke 9:10-17; John 6:1–14

"Hurry, wake up, get dressed," papa called to the boy. "Today we are going on an adventure."

The young boy's heart raced with excitement as he jumped up from his mat. He tied his cloak around him as he ran to the table. Bread and goat cheese, along with some dates, olives, and figs, awaited him. As the boy ate his breakfast, mama was busy packing lunch for each member of the family.

Papa explained. "Today, we are going to see the Master Rabbi, Jesus. News has spread that He and His disciples have come, and we can hear all the wonderful stories He tells."

Trying to hide his disappointment, a forced smile grew across the boy's face. Tucking the lunch mama wrapped for him in the folds of his cloak, his mind wandered off on the adventures he hoped for. The boy dreamed of sailing on the Sea of Galilee. As the wind pulled on the sails, he held on with all his might. He could smell the water and feel the breeze across his face as he and his papa cast out a net to catch fish for supper. His thoughts turned to an adventurous hike up the mountains, clinging to the rock walls as he pulled himself up. Anything would be better than listening to another rabbi.

The air carried the scent of wildflowers and ancient olive trees as the family approached the open field on the shore of the Sea of Galilee. A crowd, larger than the boy had ever seen, had already gathered. The distant call of birds seemed to add a melody to the murmur of the people. Sitting obediently on the grass with his family, the boy quietly listened as Jesus spoke. His voice was tender and compassionate, unlike other rabbis the boy had heard. And he had to admit, His stories were most interesting.

Before long, the cool breeze from the sea and the sparkling sunlight dancing across the water distracted him. Every wave of the sea seemed to reach out to him, calling him to come. Yielding to the temptation, he slips away to play.

Wading in the shallow water along the shore, he kicked at the waves as if trying to send them back to where they came. He saw other boys skipping stones across the sea and he hurried to join them.

The minutes turned into hours as he played in the water. Exhausted, he laid on the shore to rest and let his clothes dry. His cloak was still damp when he spied the rock formations along the foothills. Recuperated from his brief nap, he hurried to the hillside, full of energy.

With an adventurous spirit, the boy imagined himself as the leader of an expedition, exploring all the crevices and caverns. Like a playful mountain goat, he hopped from one moss-covered boulder to another. His bare feet navigated the rough terrain with ease.

As the boy climbed higher up the rocky incline, he could see the expanse of the Sea of Galilee stretching to the

4

horizon. Sitting on a ledge, he watched the fishermen's boats on the water below. He imagined himself as the captain of the boat, barking orders as his crew pulled in a large catch of fish.

From high atop a mountain ledge, he could see far across the sea. The sun that once sparkled on the water was slowly descending to the other side. Climbing from his perch, he wondered how he would find his parents in the mass of people gathered below him.

As the boy made his way down, his stomach grumbled. Realizing amid all the activity, he didn't eat his lunch. Searching through the folds of his cloak, he pulled out the lunch his mama had prepared. Just as he was about to eat, a man approached him.

"Come with me," he said. "The Master has need of you."

Taking him to Jesus, *Andrew, Simon Peter's brother, said to him, "There's a boy here who has five barley loaves and two fish—but what are they for so many?"* (John 6:8-9).

As the boy looked at Jesus, he saw a gentle, kind face and eyes filled with love.

A multitude of conflicting emotions filled the boy's heart. A sense of guilt washed over him for playing the day away instead of sitting and listening. Yet deep down, he felt forgiven. His stomach hurt with hunger, yet he knew he needed to give all that he had. He wanted to run and find his parents, but he never felt so much at home and at peace standing next to Jesus.

A tear trickled down the boy's cheek as the corners of his mouth turned into the biggest smile. Reaching out both hands, he offered Jesus the lunch his mama had made. Jesus told the disciples to have the people sit down. *Then Jesus took the loaves, and after giving thanks he distributed them to those who were seated—so also with the fish, as much as they wanted* (John 6:11).

In a crowd of thousands stood a little boy, unnoticed by the majority. No one in the crowd would have thought this boy mattered. No one would have imagined his small, insignificant gift could make a difference. But as evening approached, this little boy still had his lunch, and he selflessly gave what little he had. Jesus used his gift to perform the only miracle recorded in all four Gospels.

Little did the mama realize, God would use the work of her hands that morning to feed thousands. She didn't know Jesus would use the simple food from her kitchen to create a feast on the shore for so many. We never know what God can do with our little something.

From the examples of the little boy and his mama, we see the power of simple acts of kindness and faith. When we offer the humble gifts of our time, talents, or treasures, God will bless and multiply them beyond our imagination. He can use even the smallest offering to do amazing things.

We never know what God will ask of us, or when He will ask. We may never see how the Lord will redeem our little bits and pieces and use them to give comfort and grace to those in need. But when we give with a willing heart, He can use us to bring about miracles in the lives of others.

Prayer:
Dear Heavenly Father, forgive us for times when we may have thought we were insignificant, or our offerings were too small to make a difference. Thank You for the example of the little boy who shared his lunch and his mama who prepared it. May Your Holy Spirit inspire within us the desire to offer ourselves to You, and watch as You turn our gifts into blessings for others. In the Name of Jesus, Your Son, we pray. Amen.

Action Steps Date _____

How have you encountered Jesus Christ through today's story?

_____

_____

_____

_____

_____

Based on this story in scripture, what is God calling you to do? In what ways can you demonstrate this?

_____

_____

_____

_____

_____

What are practical ways we can help others develop Christ-like behavior?

_____

_____

_____

_____

_____

Obediently Serving God

John 2:1-12

The autumn evening was cool and delightful as the spectacular torchlight parade wound its way through the narrow cobblestone streets. Shouts of joyous celebration and resounding trumpets were heard throughout the city of Cana. The wedding ceremony had ended earlier in the evening and at the bride's home, speeches made, and expressions of goodwill were publicly declared. The festive crowd now made its way to the groom's home. There would be music and dancing, with food for everyone and free-flowing wine. Hospitality was emphasized, and the groom's family took great care to provide whatever the guests needed. The celebration would last all week, provided they could avoid the looming disaster.

The festivities proceeded as planned, and everyone enjoyed the celebration. But then the error was discovered. Despite all the careful planning, there was not adequate wine for the banquets. A cause that would certainly disgrace the groom and his family and possibly bring legal action against them.

In what should have been one of the happiest occasions of her life, Mary, a recent widow, now faced a dilemma she was unprepared to handle. In the past, Joseph would deal with such a crisis, but now she is the one responsible. Without a solution in sight, she turns to her eldest son Jesus for His help and tells the servants she hired for the event to follow His instructions. *When the wine ran out, Jesus's mother told him, "They don't have any wine." ... "Do whatever he tells you," his mother told the servants* (John 2:3,5)

Jesus tells the servants to fill six stone jars with water, each holding twenty or thirty gallons. Jesus doesn't pray over the jars or touch them. He doesn't taste the water to be certain it turned to wine. He simply tells the servants to draw some out and give it to the master of the feast.

Imagine what the servants must have been thinking? "We just filled these jars with water, and now You want us to give some to our boss who is expecting wine? Are You trying to get us fired?" But these humble servants were obedient and did what Jesus asked.

When the headwaiter tasted the water (after it had become wine), he did not know where it came from—though the servants who had drawn the water knew. He called the groom and told him, "Everyone sets out the fine wine first, then, after people are drunk, the inferior. But you have kept the fine wine until now" (John 2:9-10).

While those in attendance were unaware of the mighty working of God, these humble servants were used by God and witnessed the first miracle of Jesus, known only to them and the few disciples.

Certainly, Jesus turning water into wine solved the temporary problem at the wedding, but John lets us know there was a greater purpose. He concludes this narrative of the wedding feast with an explanation for the event. *Jesus did this, the first of his signs, in Cana of Galilee. He revealed his glory, and his disciples believed in him* (John 2:11). It was a sign to manifest His glory, and John says that as a result, His disciples believed in Him.

The servants at the wedding feast provide a powerful example for us to follow.

The Servants were Humble

The servants, in their humble service, played a crucial role in the unfolding miracle. They were humble and obedient in carrying out their duties without seeking recognition. They didn't question the unconventional solution of filling jars with water when wine was expected. Their humble service reflects Jesus' example of humility and the Christian principle of serving others.

We cannot underestimate the value of humble service. Adopting a servant-hearted attitude allows believers to serve others without seeking personal glory. Humble acts of kindness create a positive impact on others and allow them to see the power of God.

Do nothing out of selfish ambition or conceit, but in humility consider others as more important than yourselves. Everyone should look not to his own interests, but rather to the interests of others. Adopt the same attitude as that of Christ Jesus, who, existing in the form of God, did not consider equality with God as something to be exploited. Instead he emptied himself by assuming the form of a servant, taking on the likeness of humanity. And when he had come as a man, he humbled himself by becoming obedient to the point of death—even to death on a cross. (Philippians 2:3-8)

The Servants were Obedient

Mary told the servants, *"Do whatever he tells you"* (John 2:5). The servants could not understand how water could turn into wine, but they obeyed Jesus' instructions without questioning. Their obedience, even though it seemed impractical, paved the way for Jesus to display His glory.

How much better our lives would be today if we followed Mary's instructions? Christians are encouraged to face life's challenges with faithful obedience, believing Jesus can turn our struggles into amazing demonstrations of His power. Our obedient service to God results in Him being honored and glorified and causes others to believe in Him. Knowing God's Word alone is insufficient. We must obediently do what it says.

Be doers of the word and not hearers only, deceiving yourselves. Because if anyone is a hearer of the word and not a doer, he is like someone looking at his own face in a mirror. For he looks at himself, goes away, and immediately forgets what kind of person he was. But the one who looks intently into the perfect law of freedom and perseveres in it, and is not a forgetful hearer but a doer who works—this person will be blessed in what he does. (James 1:22-25)

The Servants Trusted Jesus

When Jesus told the servants to fill the jars with water, *they filled them to the brim* (John 2:7). Then, Jesus told them to *draw some out and take it to the headwaiter. And they did* (John 2:8). The servants at the wedding experienced the joy of witnessing Jesus' miraculous provision because they trusted Jesus without question.

The servant's example emphasizes the importance of trusting Jesus with our challenges and difficulties. It encourages believers to have faith in God's ability to provide beyond our expectations. We are to trust that He can turn ordinary situations into extraordinary displays of His grace.

Trust in the Lord with all your heart, and do not rely on your own understanding; in all your ways know him, and he will make your paths straight. (Proverbs 3:5-6)

The person who trusts in the Lord, whose confidence indeed is the Lord, is blessed. He will be like a tree planted by water: it sends its roots out toward a stream, it doesn't fear when heat comes, and its foliage remains green. It will not worry in a year of drought or cease producing fruit. (Jeremiah 17:7-8)

The story of the wedding at Cana encourages believers to trust in God and live in obedience to His Word. The wedding servants' example should guide and inspire Christians in our journey of faith and service. How much better we would be if we responded to Jesus, as these humble servants did. Without questioning the motive or doubting the results, seek and follow the clear teachings of Scripture and obediently serve God.

Prayer:

Dear Father, we come humbly into Your presence by the authority of Your Son, Jesus Christ, our Lord and Savior. Forgive us for the times we lacked an understanding of how You could meet our needs and we failed to be obedient to You. May we learn from these humble servants who did not doubt or question Jesus. With the prospect of embarrassment and dishonor from their master for serving water instead of wine, they faithfully and obediently carried out His instructions. May Your Holy Spirit inspire within us the desire to be faithful, obedient servants for Your Kingdom, bringing You honor and glory. In Christ's name, we pray. Amen.

Action Steps

Date _____

How have you encountered Jesus Christ through today's story?

_____

_____

_____

_____

_____

Based on this story in scripture, what is God calling you to do? In what ways can you demonstrate this?

_____

_____

_____

_____

_____

What are practical ways we can help others develop Christ-like behavior?

_____

_____

_____

_____

_____

Loving Friends

Mark 2:1-12; Luke 5:17-25

Early in the morning, a mob of people clustered around His home. As the door opened, they poured into the house, filling the rooms beyond capacity. The remaining people surrounded the home, blocking the doorway and leaning in the windows. This was not an angry mob of people, but a joyful multitude welcoming Him home.

Jesus began His ministry, preaching and teaching in the synagogue in Capernaum. He spent time there teaching and healing many who were sick with various diseases. Then, without warning, early one morning, He and His disciples left to preach in all the neighboring towns throughout Galilee (Mark 1:21-45).

Now Jesus had returned to Capernaum, and word of His return spread quickly. Thrilled by the news, they did not wait for an invitation to see Him, nor did they wait for Him to return to the synagogue on the Sabbath. Instead, they gathered at the home where He was staying.

What an example for us to follow. Are we that eager to hear God's Word preached? Jesus said, *Blessed are those who hunger and thirst for righteousness* (Matthew 5:6).

17

Today, Christians have greater access to the Bible than any time in history, but do we hunger and thirst for the truth it contains?

As Jesus taught the standing room only crowd, it happened. At first, it was just a little noise outside, some muffled voices heard above them. Then dust and debris started falling from the ceiling. The noise grew louder, and larger pieces of the roof fell on them. Before long, sunlight was shining through a hole in the roof. Everyone could clearly see four pairs of hands silhouetted against the bright blue sky, pulling the roof apart.

By now, everyone focused their attention on the roof. And just as they could distinguish four men, it became dark. A mat covered the hole, blocking the sunlight. Slowly, carefully, the mat descended. To everyone's astonishment, when it reached the floor directly in front of the teacher, there was a paralyzed man on the mat. Jesus paused as the distracted audience watched the motionless man, and above him, his four friends straining to hold on to the ropes. *Seeing their faith, Jesus told the paralytic, "Son, your sins are forgiven." ... Immediately he got up, took the mat, and went out in front of everyone* (Mark 2:5,12).

We do not know the names of the four men who brought their paralyzed friend to Jesus or anything about them. While their friend went home rejoicing that Jesus healed him, we don't know what happened to them. But I imagine they spent the rest of the day repairing the roof they had just destroyed.

Because of the faith of this remarkable group of friends, the life of this unnamed paralytic was forever changed. Through the power of Jesus, he found both physical and spiritual healing. The crowd hindered them from reaching Jesus, but their love for their friend compelled these men to overcome the obstacles and dare to do the unthinkable. Willing to risk injury climbing on the roof and being arrested

18

for vandalism, they went to remarkable lengths to help a friend in need.

The faith of these friends must have brought a smile to Jesus' face. They could have easily given up. After all, they tried their best to help their friend. They carried him to Jesus, but the task slowed them down and they were too late. It wasn't their fault there was such a large crowd, and Jesus was already busy. Besides, trying to help their friend caused them to miss Jesus' teaching.

But for these four faithful men, their friendship did not allow them to give up. It caused them to do the unexpected, the unconventional. And Jesus stood and applauded their faith. If not with His hands, He applauded with His heart. *Seeing their faith, Jesus told the paralytic, "Son, your sins are forgiven"* (Mark 2:5). The men wanted Jesus to heal their friend. But Jesus, so moved by their faith, did not settle for simply healing the body. He went beyond the physical and dealt with the spiritual. Before He healed the man's body, Jesus spoke peace to his heart, announcing He forgave the man's sins.

What an example and encouragement these four unnamed men are for us today. Each of us needs to have a few loving friends who regularly encourage us spiritually. God never intended for us to live independent lives. We are to depend on the friendship of others.

As God was creating all things, He said, *"It is not good for the man to be alone"* (Genesis 2:18). The creation of Eve was the beginning of human companionship. The Bible is full of faithful friends encouraging one another. Among them are:

> ➢ Daniel had Shadrach, Meshach, and Abednego.
> ➢ Naomi had Ruth.
> ➢ David had Jonathan.
> ➢ Paul had Timothy and Titus.

Billy Graham said, "The human soul is a lonely thing. It must have the assurance of companionship. Left entirely to itself, it cannot enjoy anything." [i]

If we are too busy for people, then we are busier than God intended us to be. God does not desire for us to live our lives alone, unconcerned for one another. He made us to need a friend to refresh our hearts and to share our burdens.

Two are better than one because they have a good reward for their efforts. For if either falls, his companion can lift him up; but pity the one who falls without another to lift him up. Also, if two lie down together, they can keep warm; but how can one person alone keep warm? And if someone overpowers one person, two can resist him. A cord of three strands is not easily broken. (Ecclesiastes 4:9-12)

Friendship is truly one of the greatest gifts in life.

Jesus said, t*his is my command: Love one another as I have loved you. No one has greater love than this: to lay down his life for his friends. You are my friends if you do what I command you. I do not call you servants anymore, because a servant doesn't know what his master is doing. I have called you friends, because I have made known to you everything I have heard from my Father.* (John 15:12-15)

We exemplify the love of Jesus when we befriend others and love them with a deep, abiding love.

Above all, maintain constant love for one another, since love covers a multitude of sins. Be hospitable to one another without complaining. Just as each one has received a gift, use it to serve others, as good stewards of the varied grace of God. (1 Peter 4:8-10)

Do nothing out of selfish ambition or conceit, but in humility consider others as more important than yourselves. Everyone should look not to his own interests, but rather to the interests of others. (Philippians 2:3-4)

Certainly, as Christians, our strength, hope, and joy comes from the Lord, but we still need the companionship and encouragement of our friends. When the Apostle Paul was alone in prison, he reached out to his friend Timothy, pleading for him to *make every effort to come to me soon ... bring Mark with you, for he is useful to me ... come before winter* (2 Timothy 4:9,11,21).

What a moving depiction of how important human touch is to our lives. Like Adam in the garden, it's not good for us to be alone. We need the companionship and encouragement of a friend. Friends for us to serve and to be served.

Let us consider one another in order to provoke love and good works, not neglecting to gather together, as some are in the habit of doing, but encouraging each other, and all the more as you see the day approaching. (Hebrews 10:24-25)

Prayer:
Dear Father, we thank You for creating friends. May we strive to follow the example of these four men, putting the interest of a friend ahead of our own. May Your Spirit develop within us a desire to love others, as these four did, compelled to overcome any obstacles in our way to meet their needs. In the name of Jesus, our friend and Your only begotten Son, who taught us to love, we pray. Amen.

---

[i] https://www.billygraham.ca/devotion/true-friendship

Action Steps

How have you encountered Jesus Christ through today's story?

_____

_____

_____

_____

_____

Based on this story in scripture, what is God calling you to do? In what ways can you demonstrate this?

_____

_____

_____

_____

_____

What are practical ways we can help others develop Christ-like behavior?

_____

_____

_____

_____

_____

The Courage & Wisdom of a Bold Evangelist

John 9:1-41

Hurriedly, he navigated his way through the cobblestone streets the best he could. He traveled each day in the early morning darkness, but that did not matter to him. The path he took was a familiar one. He knew every turn along the route, and he avoided the crowds of people that would soon fill the Jerusalem streets. Arriving early, he was hopeful of securing one of the better places to sit outside the temple gate.

But he stopped long enough to smell the fragrant beauty of the wildflowers. He whistled along with the chirping birds, thinking about what a wonderful world God had created. As he spread his blanket and took his seat, little did he realize this day would forever change his life.

Later that day, Jesus and His disciples passed by this man who was born blind. He never saw the beauty of a sunset or the grandeur of the mountains. As a child, he never saw his mother's face or the love in her eyes. But on this day, he met Jesus, who not only brought sight to his eyes but revealed to him the Light of the World.

Seeing the blind man, Jesus *spit on the ground, made some mud from the saliva, and spread the mud on his eyes. "Go," he told him, "wash in the pool of Siloam" (which means "Sent"). So he left, washed, and came back seeing* (John 9:6-7).

As he came out of the water, he saw a sparkle of light as the sun's reflection danced across the drops of water on his face. Incredible joy filled every fiber of his being as he opened his eyes. Awestruck by the breathtaking view before him left him speechless. For the first time, he could see the people around him and the expressions on their faces. The grandeur of the city buildings was more impressive than he ever dreamed.

As he made his way home, he smelled the sweet fragrance of the flowers he so often enjoyed. Turning, he saw their magnificent display of beautiful colors. He felt the bark on a tree trunk and gazed in amazement at the branches and leaves stretching high above the houses. He saw the wind blowing the limbs back and forth as if they were waving hello to him. Tasting a fig, he laughed to himself, thinking, "some things looked better in my imagination."

Quickly, he ducked out of the way as something flew past him. A smile grew across his face as he heard the familiar chirping of the birds. He stood and admired them, watching as they soared high above him. The azure blue sky filled with white billowy clouds provided a backdrop beyond anything he could have envisioned.

A deep sense of gratitude filled his heart with the greatness of God. Now, he could finally see what he had only heard, smelled, tasted, or felt. A sense of awe overcame him as he stood in wonder and admiration of the beauty of the world God created. But soon, the reality of people's cruelty would rear its ugly head.

Whatever this man's joy was, it was short-lived. First, his neighbors debated whether he was the man they knew who was born blind. The man kept insisting it was him, but they wanted proof. They demanded an explanation.

I love the man's answer. He didn't go to church and take an eight-week class on how to witness to your neighbors. Nor did he study Christian apologetics to be prepared to answer their questions. He simply testified to what he knew. *"The man called Jesus made mud, spread it on my eyes, and told me, 'Go to Siloam and wash.' So when I went and washed I received my sight"* (John 9:11).

His neighbors asked him where this Jesus was. He replied, *"I do not know"* (John 9:12b). How could he know where anything was? He had never seen anywhere before!

If their interrogation wasn't enough, his neighbors then took him to the Pharisees. Here was a man who had only envisioned the gift of sight being questioned and humiliated by those with sight, but who had no vision.

The Pharisees asked him how he could see. He simply responded, *"He put mud on my eyes, I washed, and I can see"* (John 9:15b). The Pharisees were outraged! Not because the man was healed of blindness, but because Jesus had the audacity to do it on the Sabbath!

Next, the man's parents were called in and questioned. Unfortunately for this man, his parents feared the Pharisees more than they loved their son. They told them, *"He is of age; ask him"* (John 9:23b).

They summoned the man born blind a second time, and the Pharisees continued to badger and ridicule him. They ask him how he was healed. I love the man's answer, what courage he displayed. *"I already told you,"* he said, *"and you didn't listen. Why do you want to hear it again? You don't want to become his disciples too, do you?"* (John 9:27).

The Pharisees chastised him, but the man never backed down. *"This is an amazing thing!" the man told them. "You don't know where he is from, and yet he opened my eyes. We know that God doesn't listen to sinners, but if anyone is God-fearing and does his will, he listens to him. Throughout history no one has ever heard of someone opening the eyes of a person born blind. If this man were not from God, he wouldn't be able to do anything"* (John 9:30-33).

This man knew his Bible. Nowhere in the Old Testament was anyone ever healed of blindness. Even though he was blind, he had studied the Scriptures. He knew the laws and prophets and the history of his nation. He understood the many attributes of God, the Father of Abraham, Isaac, and Jacob.

Hearing that the Pharisees had cast the man out of the temple, Jesus sought and found the man. Jesus asked him, *"Do you believe in the Son of Man?"*

"Who is he, Sir, that I may believe in him?" he asked.

Jesus answered, "You have seen him; in fact, he is the one speaking with you." "I believe, Lord!" he said, and he worshiped him (John 9:35-38).

Jesus first gave him physical sight and now he received spiritual sight, and the man believed and worshiped Him. Notice the progression of the man's understanding of Jesus. He called Him:

➢ *the man* (v. 11)
➢ *a prophet* (v. 17)
➢ *from God* (v. 33)
➢ *Lord* (v. 38)

He saw what the Pharisees never did. Truly, this man born blind, sees more than the Pharisees.

28

Prayer:

Dear Father, forgive us for all the times, like the neighbors, we doubt and question what You have done. For all the times, like the Pharisees, we exhibit physical sight and hang onto our personal preferences and traditions rather than seek spiritual wisdom. May we, like this man born blind, have the courage and strength to testify to others all You have done for us. Help us to boldly share Your light and life with all who we know. May our eyes always be open to spiritual truths so that we can truly see the majesty of Your Grace. In Christ's name, we pray. Amen.

Action Steps

How have you encountered Jesus Christ through today's story?

_____

_____

_____

_____

_____

Based on this story in scripture, what is God calling you to do? In what ways can you demonstrate this?

_____

_____

_____

_____

_____

What are practical ways we can help others develop Christ-like behavior?

_____

_____

_____

_____

_____

Giving from the Heart

Mark 12:41–44, Luke 21:1–4

Filled with loneliness and despair, she lived in a humble dwelling on the outskirts of Jerusalem. Losing her husband left her with no means of support. Every day was a struggle. Her physical and emotional burdens seemed overwhelming. Yet her faith and devotion to God never wavered.

Nearby, Jesus was teaching the people and debating with the Sadducees. As He spoke, many rich people coming to bring their offerings distracted them. They adorned themselves in their finest robes and jewels for all to envy. Filled with pride, they dropped their coins, making certain they rang loudly as they fell, drawing attention to their generous gifts.

Amid this display of affluence, the widow entered the temple, unnoticed by most. In her tattered robe, she timidly approached. With trembling hands, she quietly placed two small coins in the treasury. Barely worth anything, they were all she had. She could have kept the coins for herself, providing temporary relief from her hardships. But her heart was filled with a deep devotion to God and a desire to honor Him in every aspect of her life.

Turning to His disciples, Jesus said, *Truly I tell you, this poor widow has put more into the treasury than all the others. For they all gave out of their surplus, but she out of her poverty has put in everything she had—all she had to live on* (Mark 12:43-44).

The widow's story serves as a gentle rebuke to the prideful who seek recognition for their generosity. Jesus taught us *when you give to the poor, don't let your left hand know what your right hand is doing, so that your giving may be in secret. And your Father who sees in secret will reward you* (Matthew 6:3-4).

Jesus uses a memorable figure of speech to illustrate that our charitable deeds should be for the Father, and not to gain notoriety for the giver. Genuine giving is an act of love, not a show of personal gain or self-righteousness. Those who want others to know how generous they are receive their reward, the praise of the people. God blesses those who give from the heart. His blessings are not always monetary or material goods, but are always worth far more than we gave.

Jesus saw beyond the surface. He recognized the true motive of the widow's offering. Despite her circumstances, she surrendered everything to God, knowing He is the ultimate provider. God doesn't measure the size of our gifts, but the condition of our hearts. He values our intentions more than the amount we give.

Each person should do as he has decided in his heart— not reluctantly or out of compulsion, since God loves a cheerful giver. (2 Corinthians 9:7)

Our giving is to come from the heart, and the motive in the heart must please God. We are not to give reluctantly or begrudgingly. But give as one who cheerfully shares what we have because we have experienced the grace of God.

34

Imagine for a moment that a man gives his wife a birthday gift, and the wife responds, "Oh, how beautiful. You are so wonderful that you would give me such a precious gift." What would you think if the man said, "Don't mention it. Today is your birthday and as your husband, it is my duty to give you a gift."

How much different it would be if he said, "You are welcome. There is nothing I'd rather do than give you gifts because I love you so much. There is no one on earth I rather spend time with and do things for than you."

It is the same gift. But duty motivates one, love motivates the other. And the motive makes all the difference!

In the same way, God wants us to give, not as a formality or an obligation, but as the overflow of your love for Him. We are to give not out of duty or showmanship, but with a sincere heart. The amount of our gift is not as important as the depth of our faith and the genuineness of our devotion to God.

There are 4 Types of Giving:
➤ Grudge Giving—I have to
➤ Guilt Giving—I ought to
➤ Duty Giving—I need to
➤ Thanks Giving—I want to

What is your motive? The Apostle Paul said our giving is to be *overflowing in many expressions of thanks to God* (2 Corinthians 9:12).

The story of the widow's offering challenges us to examine our motives and encourages us to live a life of thanksgiving and generosity. Giving is not to be something we do, but something we are. It is to be the way of life for a Christian who understands the grace of God.

Prayer:

Dear Heavenly Father, forgive us for the times we may have given out of wrong motives. We thank You for including the story of this widow in Scripture. May it motivate us as we seek to love and serve You, and inspire within us a desire to live lives of selfless devotion and humble generosity. May we always be willing to surrender our possessions, time, and talents to You, even when it seems like we have little to offer. In the name of Jesus, we pray. Amen.

Action Steps

How have you encountered Jesus Christ through today's story?

_____

_____

_____

_____

_____

Based on this story in scripture, what is God calling you to do? In what ways can you demonstrate this?

_____

_____

_____

_____

_____

What are practical ways we can help others develop Christ-like behavior?

_____

_____

_____

_____

_____

The Faithful
Disciple Maker

Luke 13:6-9

His skin was dark and wrinkled from the long hours of work in the scorching sun. His fingers and hands were hard and calloused from tilling the soil. For years, he meticulously tended to each of the precious grape vines that grew in the vineyard like a father would care for his children. Carefully, he loosens the soil around the base of the plant, fertilizes and waters the vines so that they would produce a full harvest for the owner of the vineyard.

There also were fig trees throughout the vineyard among the grapevines. The trees would flourish in the rich fertile soil providing the owner a second crop, increasing his profits. In addition, the long leafy branches of the mature fig tree would provide welcomed shade for the weary workers.

Each year before the harvest, the owner of the vineyard would come and inspect his crop. This year he found the servant busy working the soil near a barren fig tree. His fingers wrapped around the long handle of the hoe as he struck the dirt. Blow after careful blow loosening the soil, allowing the moisture of the evening dew and late rains to seep in.

Seeing the barren fig tree, the owner *told the vineyard worker, 'Listen, for three years I have come looking for fruit on this fig tree and haven't found any. Cut it down! Why should it even waste the soil?* (Luke 13:7).

According to Jewish Law, fruit from newly planted trees was not to be eaten for three years. Then the fourth year, the fruit was to be given as an offering to God. A farmer could not gather figs until the fifth year.

> *When you come into the land and plant any kind of tree for food, you are to consider the fruit forbidden. It will be forbidden to you for three years; it is not to be eaten. In the fourth year all its fruit is to be consecrated as a praise offering to the Lord. But in the fifth year you may eat its fruit.* (Leviticus 19:23-25)

For the past three years, this man had expected to harvest figs from his tree. He had now been waiting seven years to receive a harvest from the tree.

The servant, however, saw beyond the barren branches. With a voice filled with compassion, he pleaded, *Sir, leave it this year also, until I dig around it and fertilize it. Perhaps it will produce fruit next year, but if not, you can cut it down* (Luke 13:8-9). The master, swayed by the servant's plea, granted permission. Like a shepherd caring for a wayward sheep, the servant set to work. He nurtured the fig tree, hopeful the extra attention would give it another chance to fulfill its purpose of bearing fruit.

The Tree in the Vineyard

In this parable, the owner is the Lord Jesus, and the vineyard represents His church. Notably, the fig tree is not a stray tree alongside the road. The owner planted the fig tree in the vineyard. It's not symbolic of a wayward person outside the church, but a believer within the church.

We must examine our own lives, ensuring we bear the fruit of the Spirit. The Apostle Paul wrote, *the fruit of the Spirit is love, joy, peace, patience, kindness, goodness, faithfulness, gentleness, and self-control* (Galatians 5:22-23). Are we like the barren tree, just taking in the Word of God fed to us, but not letting the Holy Spirit develop His fruit in us?

On the night He was betrayed, Jesus told His disciples, *My Father is glorified by this: that you produce much fruit and prove to be my disciples* (John 15:8). God desires Christians to produce much fruit of the Spirit. Like the tree in the vineyard, we consistently need to hear the Word of God taught, and our faith needs nurturing.

Are we part of a local "vineyard" where we are being fed the Word of God and discipled to spiritual maturity? Do others see evidence of the fruit of the Spirit in our lives?

The Work of the Servant

We also learn of the faithful servant, pleading with his master to give him one more year to nurture this tree. Just as the servant tended the fig tree, believers are called to invest in the lives of others. The Apostle Paul wrote, *what you have heard from me in the presence of many witnesses, commit to faithful men who will be able to teach others also* (2 Timothy 2:2). First, we must be taught and discipled in our faith. Then we are to build in the lives of others to nurture them to spiritual maturity.

Earlier in His ministry, Jesus taught the "Parable of the Sower". In it, Jesus explained the soil was like the hearts of people and the seed sown is the Word of God. The result of a spiritual crop depends on the condition of the heart. (Luke 8:4-15)

The Apostle Paul told the church at Corinth, *I planted, Apollos watered, but God gave the growth* (1 Corinthians 3:6-7). Paul sowed the seeds of the Gospel, and Apollos came after him and watered what he planted. When the work is done to prepare the soil of a person's heart, then God can bring forth spiritual growth.

As servants of God, Christians are to be faithful in their work to nurture people and to pray for them. We need to nurture, disciple, teach, and encourage one another. Then God will provide fruitful, meaningful, and abundant growth.

In a world that often demands instant results, God encourages believers to embrace the perspective of His timing. We are to nurture spiritual growth with patience and persistence, and trust God's plan for each individual.

This faithful vineyard worker pleaded with the owner to delay cutting down the fig tree to give him more time to nurture it. As Christians, how many of us plead with God to give us more time to nurture the faith of others, time to witness to one more person, time to disciple one more?

Jesus left the parable open-ended. Did the tree finally bear fruit? Did the special care accomplish anything? Was the tree spared or cut down? We have no way to know the answer to these questions, but we can answer for our own lives. The question is not, what happened to the tree, but what will happen to me? Let's not be like this tree just taking up space. But rather, let's be a servant, making disciples for God's glory.

The last words of Jesus were, *go and make disciples* (Matthew 28:19). Throughout His ministry, Jesus built into the lives of men and women. After His ascension, one hundred and twenty of His disciples met together in the upper room (Acts 1:12-15). Jesus was a disciple maker and in His final words He commanded us to do likewise.

Prayer:

Dear Heavenly Father, we come again before Your Throne by the authority given to us by Your Son, Jesus Christ. We thank You for the parables He taught us, and desire to produce much fruit for Your glory. Forgive us for the times we failed to encourage one another and nurture their faith. May Your Holy Spirit inspire us to be more like this faithful servant. Cultivating the mission field to bring forth an abundant spiritual harvest. Pleading for more time to reach just one more. In Christ's name, we pray. Amen.

Action Steps

How have you encountered Jesus Christ through today's story?

_____

_____

_____

_____

_____

Based on this story in scripture, what is God calling you to do? In what ways can you demonstrate this?

_____

_____

_____

_____

_____

What are practical ways we can help others develop Christ-like behavior?

_____

_____

_____

_____

_____

The Kingdom Builders

Matthew 25:14-30

A wise, and wealthy landowner respected for his shrewd business insight and generous heart had built a large kingdom for his family. The master was departing for a long journey, uncertain of when he would return. He summoned three respected servants to distribute talents of gold, a currency of immense value. *To one, he gave five talents, to another two talents, and to another one talent, depending on each one's ability* (Matthew 25:14-15).

As the master left on his journey, the two servants who had received five and two talents immediately set to work. With the weight of responsibility on their shoulders, they felt a mixture of excitement and apprehension. With diligence and wisdom, they used their talents for the good of their master, working to build his kingdom. They set out to invest, trade, and work diligently. Days turned into weeks, and weeks into months. Their hands were calloused from hard work, but their hearts were filled with anticipation as they saw their assets multiply.

After a long time the master of those servants came and settled accounts with them (Matthew 25:19). The first servant presented ten talents, a double return on the trust placed in him. Although the second servant's endeavors were not as extensive as the first, he also doubled his talents. Their faces beamed with satisfaction as they welcomed their master home.

They each doubled the amount given, and each received the same reward, the praise of their master. *His master said to him, "Well done, good and faithful servant! You were faithful over a few things; I will put you in charge of many things. Share your master's joy"* (Matthew 25:21, 23). It was the proportion, not the portion, that made the difference.

However, the story took a different turn for the third servant. Gripped by fear and indecision, he buried his one talent in the ground. When the master returned, the unfaithful servant dug up the talent and returned it unchanged.

The master's countenance shifted. With disappointment etched across his face, the master's response was stern yet just. *His master replied to him, "You evil, lazy servant! ... Take the talent from him and give it to the one who has ten talents. ... And throw this good-for-nothing servant into the outer darkness, where there will be weeping and gnashing of teeth"* (Matthew 25:26-30).

Jesus told His disciples this parable as He finished teaching them about things to come. Jesus revealed to them signs of the end of the age, the great tribulation, and His glorious return. Jesus then used parables to help prepare His disciples, and all future generations of believers, how to live until He returns.

The wealthy master is Jesus. He will soon leave the disciples to return to heaven, but after a long time, He will return. Jesus said, *I will come again and take you to myself, so that where I am you may be also. ... You have heard me tell you, "I am going away and I am coming to you"* (John 14:3, 28).

48

The servants represent all the people on earth. In the first century, the talent was the largest Hebrew unit of weight, a means to measure the amount given. God gives all humans talents and abilities in different amounts when they are born.

Like the servant with one talent, unbelievers hide theirs from the Kingdom of God. The talents and abilities God gives them at birth are not used to build His kingdom, but for personal pleasure and to glorify themselves. As a result, when the Lord returns, they will be separated from God for eternity. They will be thrown *into the outer darkness, where there will be weeping and gnashing of teeth* (Matthew 25:30).

Those who believe in Christ as their Savior and trust Him as their Lord, receive additional amounts. The Holy Spirit gives them spiritual gifts. Some receive more gifts than others, as represented by the servants receiving two and five talents. When Christians work to develop their talents, abilities, and gifts, using them to build the kingdom of God, it brings glory and honor to His Name. As the Apostle Paul wrote, *Do everything for the glory of God* (1 Corinthians 10:31).

As believers, we are called to a life of purpose and ministry that honors God. The story of the servants emphasizes our responsibility in using the gifts and talents God has given us. Faithfulness and diligence in even the smallest tasks bring blessings from God. He values our work of ministry, regardless of the quantity of talents or resources.

God gives all Christians different amounts of resources in three categories for us to utilize in building His kingdom.

The Amount of Time
God gives each one of us a different amount of time on this earth. And every believer accepts Christ at different

times in their life. Some have their whole life to serve Him, while others have but a few years.

In the parable of the workers in the vineyard (Matthew 20:1-15), some men worked all day. Some worked only half a day, and others worked only one hour, but they all got paid the same amount. What's important is not the amount we have, but how we use the time given to us.

Pay careful attention, then, to how you walk—not as unwise people but as wise—making the most of the time, because the days are evil. (Ephesians 5:15-16)

The Amount of Treasures

Some people, like King Solomon, find it easy to make money. While others, like the poor widow in Mark chapter twelve, struggle to get by. God gives some people more wealth, as shown by the servant with five talents. *Remember that the Lord your God gives you the power to gain wealth* (Deuteronomy 8:18). With it, they can support more ministries with larger offerings.

How much we have is not as important to God as what we do with what we have. Whether we have little or much, we are to *honor the Lord with your possessions and with the first produce of your entire harvest* (Proverbs 3:9).

Don't store up for yourselves treasures on earth, where moth and rust destroy and where thieves break in and steal. But store up for yourselves treasures in heaven, where neither moth nor rust destroys, and where thieves don't break in and steal. For where your treasure is, there your heart will be also. (Matthew 6:19-21)

The Amount of Talents

God gives each person unique talents and abilities, and Christians receive different spiritual gifts. Some Christians receive the ability to reach thousands of people through global ministries. Others have local ministries reaching only a few. Some have public ministries while others serve in solitude.

God desires for us to achieve the ministry He has given us. Those given two talents are not to burden themselves with not being able to use five. But those given five talents are not to be content with using only two. With greater measure comes greater responsibility. *From everyone who has been given much, much will be required; and from the one who has been entrusted with much, even more will be expected* (Luke 12:48).

> *Just as each one has received a gift, use it to serve others, as good stewards of the varied grace of God. If anyone speaks, let it be as one who speaks God's words; if anyone serves, let it be from the strength God provides, so that God may be glorified through Jesus Christ in everything.* (1 Peter 4:10-11)

Near the end of His earthly ministry, Jesus prayed, "Father, *I have glorified you on the earth by completing the work you gave me to do*" (John 17:4). We exemplify Christlikeness when we complete the work of ministry God gave us to do, and through that ministry, we give Him the glory and honor.

The two faithful servants provide a powerful example of how we can use the resources God has entrusted to us. They challenge us to step out in faith, trusting God has equipped us for a purpose. We are to be diligent in our efforts, recognizing God honors faithfulness and rewards those who use their talents to further His kingdom.

As we look forward to the return of Christ, may these kingdom-building servants inspire us to make the most of our God-given opportunities. When we faithfully use the time, treasure, and talent given to us, we will hear those precious six words from our Lord. *Well done, good and faithful servant.*

Prayer:

Dear Heavenly Father, we thank You for the teaching of Jesus preserved for us in Scripture. May the examples of these two faithful servants inspire us to fully utilize the time, treasure, and talent You have given us. As we eagerly wait for the glorious return of Your Son, may we work diligently to build Your kingdom and bring honor and glory to You. In the name of Jesus, we pray. Amen.

Action Steps

Date _____

How have you encountered Jesus Christ through today's story?

_____

_____

_____

_____

_____

Based on this story in scripture, what is God calling you to do? In what ways can you demonstrate this?

_____

_____

_____

_____

_____

What are practical ways we can help others develop Christ-like behavior?

_____

_____

_____

_____

_____

When Gratitude Overflows

Luke 17:11-19

The bright sun shone on a small village nestled among the rolling hills. The various shades of green of the grass and trees blended effortlessly with the clear blue sky. Vibrant colors of wildflowers dotted the landscape, producing a breathtaking view, and filled the air with a sweet aroma. While a sweet melody of birds singing in the breeze was heard echoing among the hills. A cool breeze from the valley below provided the needed refreshment from the sun's rays. It was as if nature itself was inviting people to explore the beauty that lay before them.

Jesus and His disciples were heading to Jerusalem, traveling between Samaria and Galilee. This was Jesus' final pilgrimage to the Holy City, the last time He would pass this way. As they approached the village, the sense of peace and serenity was abruptly shattered. Words of warning, of misery and despair, echoed throughout the countryside. A group of ten unfortunate souls gathered, calling out, "unclean, unclean," as they cautioned everyone to stay away.

They suffered from a dreaded disease that left them with disfigured skin and endless agony. The wounds and sores covering their bodies marked them as outcasts from society.

Each day was filled with physical struggle, compounded by the weight of despair. Isolated from friends and family, they clung to the comfort and companionship of each other's company.

Word spread quickly that Jesus was coming their way, and soon the entire village was abuzz with anticipation. The ten lepers heard the whispers of the crowd and the news that He had performed miracles that defied human understanding. As they glimpsed Jesus in the distance, a flicker of hope ignited within their hearts. Their bodies may have been weak, but their desperation overpowered any doubts.

With tattered clothes flapping in the wind and the pungent stench of decaying skin permeating the air, they approached Jesus. Their hearts raced, their breath caught in their throats, and tears of anticipation filled their eyes. Standing at a distance, summoning every ounce of courage they had left, they called out to Jesus. Their voices quivered as they pleaded, *"Jesus, Master, have mercy on us!"* (Luke 17:13).

Overflowing with compassion, Jesus paused and turned toward them. His eyes filled with an indescribable warmth as He gazed upon their disfigured forms. He saw their suffering, their unspoken prayers, and He knew the torment they had endured. With a gentle smile, Jesus spoke. His voice resonated with kindness as He replied, *"Go and show yourselves to the priests"* (Luke 17:14).

Hope surged within their hearts as they obediently turned and followed Jesus' instructions. With each step, waves of astonishment washed over them. Looking down, they noticed their skin becoming clearer, their wounds vanishing, and the pain dissipating. Miraculously, their leprosy was fading away, and their limbs regained strength. Overwhelmed with joy, they realized they were no longer condemned to a life of isolation and suffering. The weight of their affliction had been lifted, and tears of joy streamed down their faces, washing away years of pain and anguish.

As they continued their journey, a glimmer of gratitude stirred in the heart of one leper. A feeling of indebtedness tugged at his conscience, compelling him to turn back. Ignoring the protests of his companions, he retraced his steps, his heart pounding with a sense of urgency.

A profound sense of appreciation washed over him. Gratitude for the healing he had received, for the chance at a new life, and for the Person who had brought him this miraculous gift. His heart overflowed with a depth of emotion that transcended words. Falling to his knees before Jesus, with a loud voice, he gave glory to God. In an act of true humility and genuine gratitude, he fell on his face before Jesus. His voice trembled as he thanked Him.

The other nine lepers continued their journey, rejoicing in their newfound health. They were so caught up in their own happiness they forgot to thank the Person who had made it all possible. But for the one who returned, a profound transformation occurred within his soul. As he rose to his feet, a deep sense of purpose and devotion enveloped him. He understood that his healing was not only a physical restoration but a spiritual awakening. From that day forward, he vowed to live a life of gratitude and service, forever cherishing the encounter with Jesus that had changed his life.

The story of the ten lepers reminds us of God's unfailing love and mercy. The one leper who returned to Jesus to express his gratitude serves as a powerful example for us to follow. Through him we see the importance of acknowledging and appreciating the blessings we receive. The value of being thankful cannot be overstated. Nurturing an attitude of thankfulness enriches our lives, nourishes our well-being, and brings joy into our daily lives.

Gratitude is more than just saying "thank you." It involves recognizing and appreciating the blessings we receive, expressing appreciation to others, and acknowledging the source of those blessings. Gratitude has the power to transform our perspective, shifting our focus from what we lack to what we have. It is a powerful antidote to the attitudes of entitlement, selfishness, and discontentment found in today's world.

During His ministry, Jesus consistently demonstrated His gratitude to His Heavenly Father. As we increasingly express our gratitude and appreciation towards Him, we gradually grow to resemble His character and transform into His likeness.

In our fast-paced and often self-focused world, it is easy to lose sight of the importance of expressing gratitude and thanksgiving to our Creator. Scripture instructs us to give thanks, and reminds us of the reason why.

Be filled by the Spirit: speaking to one another in psalms, hymns, and spiritual songs, singing and making music with your heart to the Lord, giving thanks always for everything to God the Father in the name of our Lord Jesus Christ. (Ephesians 5:19-21)

My soul, bless the Lord, and do not forget all his benefits. He forgives all your iniquity; he heals all your diseases. He redeems your life from the Pit; he crowns you with faithful love and compassion. He satisfies you with good things. (Psalm 103:2-5)

Be grateful to God. Give thanks—it changes things. Expressing thankfulness has the power to transform our hearts, our relationships, and our perspective. Cultivate a grateful spirit, recognizing God's goodness, faithfulness, and provision in all circumstances. Give Him thanks.

Prayer:

Dear Heavenly Father, forgive us for the times we acted like the nine lepers who did not return to give thanks. When our lives become filled with challenges and uncertainties, help us stay focused and come to You with a grateful heart for all You have done for us. May Your Holy Spirit help us follow the example of the Samaritan leper who thanked Jesus and gave You the glory for his healing. Rather than focusing on what we lack, may we always be filled with gratitude and thanksgiving for all You are to us, all You have given us, and for who we have become as believers. In the glorious name of our Lord and Savior, Jesus Christ, we pray. Amen.

Action Steps

How have you encountered Jesus Christ through today's story?

_____

_____

_____

_____

_____

Based on this story in scripture, what is God calling you to do? In what ways can you demonstrate this?

_____

_____

_____

_____

_____

What are practical ways we can help others develop Christ-like behavior?

_____

_____

_____

_____

_____

A Special Family

John 12:1-11

It seemed to be an innocent event, a quiet evening of fellowship. Yet this reunion proved to be a most insightful occasion. Jesus' eyes are fixed on Calvary. The crucifixion is only a week away, and Jesus is making His final trip to Jerusalem. But on His way, He makes a detour to make one last visit with His dear friends in Bethany. *Six days before the Passover, Jesus came to Bethany where Lazarus was, the one Jesus had raised from the dead* (John 12:1).

Seeing Martha, Mary, and their brother Lazarus must have brought special encouragement and strength to the Savior's heart. Jesus had a close affection for this family and visited them frequently throughout His ministry. Knowing this would be the last time He would see them on this earth must have brought a sadness to His heart. The heartache and sorrow His death would bring them had to weigh heavily on His mind.

As the events of the evening unfolded, John describes the last recorded acts of the three siblings. In doing so, he provides wonderful examples for all Christians to imitate.

Martha the Worker

First is Martha doing what Martha does. Jesus and His disciples are dining with her brother, and there is Martha, hard at work serving Jesus. It was Martha, unnoticed, working diligently to prepare the meal. As she enters the room, exhausted from her work, she blows a puff of air at the hair that has fallen across her face. In one swift motion, she wipes the sweat from her forehead and tucks her hair back under her head cloth.

Unfazed by having thirteen unexpected guests for dinner, Martha was the ultimate gracious host and organizer. Her steadfast devotion to making certain the dinner was prepared properly and served was just as much a fragrant offering as Mary's perfume.

As the Apostle Paul wrote about our work, *whatever you do, do it from the heart, as something done for the Lord and not for people, knowing that you will receive the reward of an inheritance from the Lord. You serve the Lord Christ.* (Colossians 3:23-24)

Mary the Worshiper

Next comes Mary, showing her devotion to Jesus through a spontaneous act of love and worship. Mary of Bethany is recorded three times in the Gospels. Each time she is in the same place, at the feet of Jesus. She sat at His feet listening to His teaching (Luke 10:39), fell at His feet expressing her sorrow (John 11:32), and kneeled at His feet, pouring out her worship (John 12:3).

Mary's focus was solely on Jesus. She wasn't distracted by those around her or worried about what they thought about her. She just sat there quietly and humbly, making Him the center of her world. It is significant to note that Mary of Bethany was not one of the women who went to the tomb to anoint the body of Jesus. She did not wait until it was too late to show her admiration. While He was still alive, she anointed Him in a beautiful act of personal worship.

We don't have to wait until Sunday to worship God. Our corporate worship on Sunday should be the climax of our personal daily worship throughout the week.

Let the whole earth sing to the Lord. Proclaim his salvation from day to day. Declare his glory among the nations, his wondrous works among all peoples. ... Worship the Lord in the splendor of his holiness. (1Chronicles 16:23-24, 29)

Lazarus the Witness

Last is their brother Lazarus. John tells us that a *large crowd of the Jews came not only because of Jesus but also to see Lazarus, the one he had raised from the dead* (John 12:9). Not only did they come to see him, but *he was the reason many of the Jews were believing in Jesus* (John 12:10).

In all of Scripture, there are no recorded words of Lazarus. However, through his witness, many people came to Jesus. Our lives speak the gospel to others. For good or bad, we influence those around us every day.

But in your hearts regard Christ the Lord as holy, ready at any time to give a defense to anyone who asks you for a reason for the hope that is in you. Yet do this with gentleness and reverence, keeping a clear conscience, so that when you are accused, those who disparage your good conduct in Christ will be put to shame. (1 Peter 3:15-16)

The examples of these precious friends of Jesus provide models of godly behavior to be developed in our Christian life. Martha worked in serving Jesus, Mary worshipped at

His feet, and Lazarus' very life was a witness to His miraculous power.

Certainly, as believers, we are to exhibit each of these characteristics in our life. It is a balance of our work, our worship, and our witness that defines our walk with God. However, just as each member of this precious family in Bethany had a unique gift, the Holy Spirit gives every member of God's family unique gifts to minister for Him. Some evangelize the lost, others disciple the saved. While some work quietly behind the scenes, others lead us in praise and worship.

The Apostle Peter, an eyewitness to the events in Bethany, wrote: *Just as each one has received a gift, use it to serve others, as good stewards of the varied grace of God. If anyone speaks, let it be as one who speaks God's words; if anyone serves, let it be from the strength God provides, so that God may be glorified through Jesus Christ in everything.* (1 Peter 4:10-11)

Prayer:

Dear Father, we are forever grateful You adopted us into Your family. We pray for the Marthas among us. Bless their service and give them strength and perseverance as they minister for You. For the Marys we pray You receive their worship. Encourage and revitalize them as they continue to praise You. And for those like Lazarus, honor their conviction and give them courage and boldness as they witness for You. Most of all, dear Lord, we pray for Your Name to be honored and glorified as we serve as good stewards of the various gifts You have given us. In Christ's name, we pray, Amen.

Action Steps

How have you encountered Jesus Christ through today's story?

_____

_____

_____

_____

_____

Based on this story in scripture, what is God calling you to do? In what ways can you demonstrate this?

_____

_____

_____

_____

_____

What are practical ways we can help others develop Christ-like behavior?

_____

_____

_____

_____

_____

Eager Hearts, Fruitful Lives

Acts 17:10-15

In the quiet of the night, they slipped out of town. Under the cover of darkness, they headed west on the main highway leading to Rome. As the first rays of the morning sun trickled through the darkness, they turned south on a little used road until they reached the ancient city of Berea. Nestled in the foothills just north of Mount Olympus, Berea was a quiet little town. For centuries, the wealthy would vacation in this resort community. Here, Paul and Silas would be safe from the riots in Thessalonica, and Timothy would join them later.

As was the Apostle Paul's custom, he entered the synagogue and proclaimed the word of God. He taught the Jewish community about Jesus. In addition, many of the prominent citizens came to hear Paul's teaching. However, it wasn't long before the Jews who started the riots in Thessalonica learned where they were located and came to stir-up trouble.

Once again, the believers had to escort them out of town for their safety. This time, they took Paul to the seaport, and he sailed alone to Athens. Silas and Timothy would circle back through Macedonia to encourage the churches they had established and bring a report to Paul. While their ministry in Berea was short-lived, what transpired there has stood as a glowing example for generations of Christians.

The Bereans were Eager to Learn

The Bereans' hearts burned with eagerness to receive the message of the Gospel. *They received the word with eagerness* (Acts 17:11). They listened to Paul with anticipation. Unlike the unbelieving Jews in Thessalonica, the Bereans were eager to hear the teaching of Paul and Silas.

The Apostle Peter wrote, *like newborn infants, desire the pure milk of the word, so that by it you may grow up into your salvation, if you have tasted that the Lord is good* (1 Peter 2:2-3). Just as a newborn baby desires milk, Christians should eagerly desire hearing God's Word taught. As the Psalmist said, *God, you are my God; I eagerly seek you. I thirst for you; my body faints for you in a land that is dry, desolate, and without water* (Psalm 63:1).

The Bereans Studied Diligently

The Bereans coupled their eagerness with diligence. *They ... examined the Scriptures daily to see if these things were so* (Acts 17:11). The Bereans were listening to the teaching of the most famous apostle and theologian of the early church. Yet, they searched the Scriptures when Paul taught, to see if his teaching was truly biblical. They would not accept Paul's teaching without checking for themselves, so they could know if these things were true.

The Apostle Paul wrote, *be diligent* [study] *to present yourself to God as one approved, a worker who doesn't need to be ashamed, correctly teaching the word of truth* (2 Timothy 2:15). The Bereans didn't merely skim through reading the Scriptures. They invested time and effort daily into understanding God's Word.

Paul told the Corinthian church *I gave you milk to drink, not solid food, since you were not yet ready for it. In fact, you are still not ready* (1 Corinthians 3:2). But in Berea, they were not content with just the milk of God's Word. They desired the meat as well. *But solid food is for the mature—for those whose senses have been trained to distinguish between good and evil* (Hebrews 5:14).

As they examined the Scriptures, their faith grew deeper roots. Their hearts were fertile ground for the seeds of God's Word to flourish. Their diligent, extended study revealed their hunger for a genuine relationship with God.

The Bereans Exercised Discernment

The Bereans did not take Paul's words at face value. They were discerning believers and understood the importance of distinguishing truth from falsehood. Their quest for truth was not driven by skepticism, but by an unwavering thirst to align their lives with Scripture. While eager to learn new truths about God, they made certain it agreed with the clear teaching of God's Word.

The Apostle John wrote, d*ear friends, do not believe every spirit, but test the spirits to see if they are from God, because many false prophets have gone out into the world* (1 John 4:1). It is easy to fall prey to those who teach about the God we want, rather than the God who is. We must be diligent to discern truth from error.

Paul's prayer for the Philippians is as relevant today as the day he wrote it. *I pray this: that your love will keep on growing in knowledge and every kind of discernment, so that you may approve the things that are superior and may be pure and blameless in the day of Christ* (Philippians 1:9-10).

Growing in the knowledge of God is an admirable trait, but we must accompany the desire to learn with discernment.

The Bereans Enjoyed Scripture

The act of examining the Scriptures daily wasn't a chore for the Bereans—it was a joy. They sought to unearth hidden treasures of divine wisdom, drawing them into a deeper connection with God. For them, the Bible was not simply a pretty book of poetry or nice spiritual inspiration for thoughts-for-the-day. It was a book of truth, which was there to be discovered through diligent study.

> *How I love your instruction! It is my meditation all day long. Your command makes me wiser than my enemies, for it is always with me. I have more insight than all my teachers because your decrees are my meditation. I understand more than the elders because I obey your precepts.* (Psalms119:97-100)

The Bereans Study was Fruitful

The result of their diligent study was a firm belief in the message of the Gospel. Many among them, both Jews and Greeks, came to faith through this process of thorough investigation. *Consequently, many of them believed, including a number of the prominent Greek women as well as men* (Acts 17:12).

The saints in Berea matured in their faith and in their service to the Lord. One man that was discipled by Paul in Berea, joined him on his third missionary journey through Greece and Macedonia. *He was accompanied by Sopater son of Pyrrhus from Berea* (Acts 20:4).

Paul had nothing to fear from the diligent searching of the Scriptures by the Bereans. If they were truly seeking God and His Word, they would find what Paul was preaching was accurate. The church at Berea is an excellent example of Jesus' words. *And those like seed sown on good ground hear the word, welcome it, and produce fruit thirty, sixty, and a hundred times what was sown.* (Mark 4:20).

An Example to Follow

When Jesus was twelve years old, His parents search for Him in Jerusalem. *After three days, they found him in the temple sitting among the teachers, listening to them and asking them questions. And all those who heard him were astounded at his understanding and his answers* (Luke 2:46-47).

The Bereans modeled that desire to search and learn from Scripture. As a result, God proclaimed, *the people here were of more noble character than those in Thessalonica* (Acts 17:11). What an example the Bereans set for us to follow.

Prayer:

Dear Father in Heaven, we thank You for including the story of the Berean church and their example in Scripture. May Your Holy Spirit develop within us such a desire to study Your Word daily. May we be discerning in what we hear taught, and search the Scriptures ourselves to discover Your truths. Help us apply Biblical knowledge in our lives so we may grow in the image of Your Son, Jesus Christ. In His name, we pray. Amen.

Action Steps

How have you encountered Jesus Christ through today's story?

_____

_____

_____

_____

_____

Based on this story in scripture, what is God calling you to do? In what ways can you demonstrate this?

_____

_____

_____

_____

_____

What are practical ways we can help others develop Christ-like behavior?

_____

_____

_____

_____

_____

A Selfless Act of Service

Acts 9:36-43

Slowly, her fingers slid along the hem of the garment. Carefully, she examined each stitch. The new robe she was creating needed to be her finest work, as it was for a very important lady. The clothes she made now were all for the most precious people. They were to be worn by the children of God, the poor widows from her household of faith who could not afford new clothes.

Lifting her hand, Tabitha, also known as Dorcas, held the needle up to the sunlight shining through the window as she threaded it. The status of the women who would wear the garments she made did not matter to her. Carefully, she cut and stitched as if the clothes were for the King of kings and Lord of lords. Because she knew deep down in her heart what the Apostle Paul would later write. *Whatever you do, do it from the heart, as something done for the Lord and not for people* (Colossians 3:23).

During His ministry, Jesus never traveled to her city of Joppa, and most likely Tabitha never met Him. But after the persecution broke out against the church in Jerusalem, Joppa became one of the earliest cities to have a Christian congregation. Those who had met Jesus taught others about what He said and did.

Joppa was a wealthy seaport and many of the new Christians, like Tabitha, looked after those who were less fortunate. As James, the half-brother of Jesus, would later write, *pure and undefiled religion before God the Father is this: to look after orphans and widows in their distress* (James 1:27). While she knew she did not have the means to help all the poor in the world, she diligently used what she had to assist the widows in her community.

But as quickly as a storm could blow in from the sea, the darkness of sorrow fell over her house. Suddenly, Tabitha became sick and died. The disciples in Joppa heard the Apostle Peter was in Lydda, a nearby city, and sent word for him to come. Maybe he could share some words of comfort to ease their sorrow.

As Peter entered the house, many from the community were there mourning her death. All the widows came and, through their tears, told him of her ministry sewing garments for them. In an impromptu fashion show, they displayed all the clothes Tabitha had made while she was with them.

Peter sent them all out of the room. He knelt down, prayed, and turning toward the body said, "Tabitha, get up." She opened her eyes, saw Peter, and sat up. He gave her his hand and helped her stand up. He called the saints and widows and presented her alive (Acts 9: 40-41).

Throughout the book of Acts, God performs miraculous works through the Apostles to validate their ministry. However, Scripture clearly states the disciples in Joppa called for Peter to come (Acts 9:38). They already knew of his authority as an apostle. Here, God performs a miraculous work not to validate the apostle but to put His stamp of approval on the selfless act of service.

Tabitha was a humble servant sewing clothes and God thinks her ministry to the church was so valuable that she needed to continue to do it. She had a special ministry to the poor widows that no one else fulfilled. And God, through Peter, raised her from the dead so she could continue her ministry in that church.

Often in the church, we view the people who teach or preach as being more precious to God. But that is not the way God sees. Ministries we rarely notice, the ones we often don't even know who performs them, are just as precious to God.

The Apostle Paul wrote, *For just as the body is one and has many parts, and all the parts of that body, though many, are one body—so also is Christ. ... God has arranged each one of the parts in the body just as he wanted. And if they were all the same part, where would the body be? As it is, there are many parts, but one body. ... those parts of the body that are weaker are indispensable. And those parts of the body that we consider less honorable, we clothe these with greater honor. ... God has put the body together, giving greater honor to the less honorable.* (1 Corinthians 12:12-25)

Certainly, we need pastors and teachers in our churches. We need to obediently follow their leadership (Hebrew 13:17) and they are worthy of their wages (Luke 10:7, & 1 Timothy 5:17-18). Their teaching is vital to our spiritual growth.

Today, with phone apps, podcasts, and the internet, we can listen to preachers twenty-four hours a day, seven days a week. But we also need to heed James' warning to *be doers of the word and not hearers only, deceiving yourselves* (James 1:22). Paul wrote, *the hearers of the law are not righteous before God, but the doers of the law will be justified* (Romans 2:13). Jesus said, *if you know these things, you are blessed if you do them* (John 13:17). Our blessing from God comes not from what we know of God's Word, but what we practice from God's Word.

The ninth chapter of Acts is a story that most Christians are very familiar with, the story of the conversion of the Apostle Paul on the Damascus Road. Then, in chapter ten, Luke records taking the gospel to the Gentiles for the first time in the wonderful story of the conversion of Cornelius. Tucked in between these two marvelous sections of Scripture is this incredible brief story of this dear lady who served the Lord with her talent. And in a powerful way, God reminds us of the ultimate value our service is to Him.

Just as each one has received a gift, use it to serve others, as good stewards of the varied grace of God. ... If anyone serves, let it be from the strength God provides, so that God may be glorified through Jesus Christ in everything. (1 Peter 4:10-11)

Regardless of what your ministry is, every single ministry in the church is essential.

Jesus said, *whoever wants to become great among you must be your servant, and whoever wants to be first among you must be your slave; just as the Son of Man did not come to be served, but to serve* (Matthew 20:28).

On the night Jesus was betrayed, He took the form of a servant and washed the disciples' feet. He then said, *I have given you an example, that you also should do just as I have done for you* (John 13:15). There is nothing we can do to emulate our Lord more fully than when our love for God and compassion for others compels us to serve them.

Now there are different gifts, but the same Spirit. There are different ministries, but the same Lord. And there are different activities, but the same God works all of them in each person. (1 Corinthians 12:4-6)

If you think your ministry is unimportant, remember Tabitha. Though she was but a seamstress, she gave her talent to the Lord and used it in such a manner that her good works have lived on long after her. There is no such thing as an insignificant ministry in the Kingdom of God.

Prayer:

Dear Father, forgive us for the times we have thought our tasks were insignificant to the body of Christ. For the times we may have thought some other person's ministry was more valuable to You. May we fully understand the body of Christ comprises many parts, and each part is important for the church to function properly. Help us see the eternal value in the ministry You have called us to perform. And may we be an encouragement to others as they tirelessly strive to serve You. In Christ's holy name, we pray. Amen.

Action Steps

How have you encountered Jesus Christ through today's story?

_____

_____

_____

_____

_____

Based on this story in scripture, what is God calling you to do? In what ways can you demonstrate this?

_____

_____

_____

_____

_____

What are practical ways we can help others develop Christ-like behavior?

_____

_____

_____

_____

_____

Forgiving the Unforgivable

Philemon

Nestled between twin peaks in a peaceful valley lies the prosperous community Colosse. Here, commerce and agriculture flourishes. Among the affluent stands Philemon, a man whose wealth extends beyond the boundaries of his flourishing estate. The flickering candles in his grand residence illuminate not only the affluent surroundings, but also the faces of those who gather to worship. Under the leadership of Philemon, his wife, Apphia, and son Archippus, the church at Colosse takes root. Within the walls of their home, believers come together to worship, pray, and study the Scriptures and teachings of the apostles.

Little did Philemon realize his life, marked by generosity and hospitality, would take an unexpected turn. His faith would soon face a profound test; his convictions tested in ways he never expected.

Onesimus, a runaway slave who had stolen money from Philemon, returns to his home carrying two letters. The first was a letter from the Apostle Paul for Philemon to read to the congregation meeting in his home. The second was a personal letter from the apostle directed to Philemon himself. In it, Paul tenderly implored his friend Philemon to receive back his disobedient slave and forgive him.

Onesimus had robbed his master and then fled to Rome, hoping to be lost in the crowded city. But, in the Providence of God, he met Paul and accepted Christ as his Savior. While in Rome, Onesimus grew in his faith. The Apostle Paul taught him from the Scriptures, and Onesimus ministered to Paul in his imprisonment.

As time passed, Paul knew if Onesimus was to continue to mature in his faith, he needed to seek forgiveness from those he wronged. Amid the flickering candlelight of his prison cell, Paul crafts a profound plea for forgiveness and reconciliation.

Memories of Onesimus flooded Philemon's thoughts. The runaway slave and thief had caused him financial loss, and bitterness threatened to take root in his heart. The law permitted a master to execute a rebellious slave, but Philemon was a Christian. If he forgave Onesimus, what would the other masters think? Would other slaves follow his lead? But if he punished him, how would it affect his Christian testimony and ministry in Colosse?

What a dilemma.

Bound by legal and social standards, yet as a believer in Christ, Philemon knew he was called to a higher standard. Scripture does not reveal the fate of Onesimus. However, from church history, we learn Onesimus received forgiveness and later followed Timothy as the bishop of the church at Ephesus. While there, he continued Timothy's work gathering and preserving the scrolls of the writings of the Apostle Paul. Onesimus was instrumental in producing the first scroll containing a collection of Paul's letters. "With this publication of the Pauline letters, the history of the New Testament, as a fixed collection of books, properly begins."[i]

The parchment scroll carried by Onesimus provided the advice Philemon needed. Paul's profound insights provide timeless lessons for believers about forgiveness, unity, and the life-changing impact of Christ.

Forgiveness Comes from the Heart

For this reason, although I have great boldness in Christ to command you to do what is right, I appeal to you, instead, on the basis of love. (Philemon 8-9)

Paul knew if commanded, Philemon would forgive Onesimus out of obligation. But bitterness and resentment could remain in Philemon's heart. True forgiveness must come freely from the heart. Paul urged Philemon to see beyond past wrongs, and allow love to triumph over the social norms of the day.

In his letter, Paul invites Philemon to break down the walls of unforgiveness and go beyond expectations by extending love and grace. It inspires believers to express the love and forgiveness exemplified by Christ.

Forgiveness Has a Cost

If he has wronged you in any way, or owes you anything, charge that to my account. I, Paul, write this with my own hand: I will repay it—not to mention to you that you owe me even your very self. (Philemon 18-19)

Forgiveness always comes at a cost to the one granting the forgiveness. Forgiving Onesimus came at a cost for Philemon. He experienced the loss of his work as a slave and the monetary value of what he had stolen. Paul tells Philemon to charge it to his account.

Forgiving someone does not erase or undo the wrong. When justice (or vengeance) is implemented, the person who hurt us pays the price. When we choose to forgive, we pay the price. The debt is charged to our account.

We are reminded of the enormous debt we had as sinners and how it was all charged to the account of the Lord Jesus at Calvary. For God to forgive sin, His Son had to pay the price of His death on the cross. We receive His righteousness, and He receives our sin. *He made the one who did not know sin to be sin for us, so that in him we might become the righteousness of God* (2 Corinthians 5:21).

Forgiveness Restores Unity

Once he was useless to you, but now he is useful both to you and to me. ... For perhaps this is why he was separated from you for a brief time, so that you might get him back permanently, no longer as a slave, but more than a slave—as a dearly loved brother. He is especially so to me, but how much more to you, both in the flesh and in the Lord. (Philemon 11-16)

Paul's focus was on genuine reconciliation rather than just resolution. Philemon not only received Onesimus back, but under better conditions than he had known before. Philemon received him not as a slave, but as a beloved brother in Christ.

In forgiving others, we are to strive to rebuild the relationship. Forgiveness is not just a single act, but a step toward restoring unity within the community of believers. Philemon and Onesimus provide an example of what true forgiveness can accomplish. The forgiving and forgiven, united in Christ for the work of ministry.

Christ Is the Example

Therefore, as God's chosen ones, holy and dearly loved, put on compassion, kindness, humility, gentleness, and patience, bearing with one another and forgiving one another if anyone has a grievance against another. Just as the Lord has forgiven you, so you are also to forgive. (Colossians 3:12-13)

As Philemon read these words to his congregation, he was reminded again of his need to forgive Onesimus. Jesus provided the example by forgiving us. In sending his former slave for restoration, Paul was asking Philemon to do what Jesus had done for him.

Throughout His ministry, Jesus set an example of forgiveness. He forgave the woman caught in adultery (John 8:2-11), the paralytic on the mat (Mark 2:1-12), the woman who anointed His feet (Luke 7:36-50), and others. He even asked for forgiveness for those who crucified Him (Luke 23:34).

The greatest test of our understanding and acceptance of God's forgiveness is whether we will forgive others. If we comprehend how much God has forgiven us and what it cost to provide that forgiveness, we will not be so reluctant to offer forgiveness to others.

Let all bitterness, anger and wrath, shouting and slander be removed from you, along with all malice. And be kind and compassionate to one another, forgiving one another, just as God also forgave you in Christ. (Ephesians 4:31-32)

An Example to Follow

Just as Philemon forgave Onesimus, Scripture encourages believers to forgive others who have wronged us. Forgiveness liberates us from the thoughts of disappointment, bitterness, and resentment, and allows God to give us the healing we need.

Forgiving others for what they have done to us or to our loved ones is one of the hardest things for us to do. Certainly, the pain and hurt are real, and the thought of forgiveness may seem impossible. But the pain of living with the burden of bitterness and unforgiveness will quench the Spirit of God in our lives and ruin our relationship with others.

Forgiveness allows the love of Christ to heal and restore the relationship. We may never know the mighty way in which God will use the person we forgive. Like Onesimus, our forgiveness may free them to serve Him in ways we could never imagine.

Prayer:
Dear Heavenly Father, we are forever grateful for Your love and forgiveness. We thank You for Paul's letter to Philemon reminding us to forgive others as You have forgiven us. Help us let go of bitterness and resentment and truly forgive others. May Your Holy Spirit inspire within us, Your divine love and compassion for others, looking beyond their past and seeing them for what they can become. In the precious name of Your Son, Jesus Christ, we pray. Amen.

[i] John Knox, *Philemon Among the Letters of Paul* (Chicago IL: The University of Chicago Press, 1935) 56-57

Action Steps

How have you encountered Jesus Christ through today's story?

_____

_____

_____

_____

_____

Based on this story in scripture, what is God calling you to do? In what ways can you demonstrate this?

_____

_____

_____

_____

_____

What are practical ways we can help others develop Christ-like behavior?

_____

_____

_____

_____

_____

Passing on the
Torch of Faith

Acts 18:24-26

As the sun immersed the city of Ephesus in its golden rays, the stage was set for an encounter that would forever change the life of a gifted speaker. The busy streets whispered tales of a charismatic orator, whose words ignited a fire within the hearts of those who heard him. Little did he know he would soon cross paths with a humble couple, whose love and wisdom would reveal a deeper understanding of the Gospel he thought he already knew.

Apollos possessed an impressive knowledge of Scripture and spoke with eloquence and clarity. He talked passionately about Jesus, the long-awaited Messiah. As he taught in the local synagogue, his wisdom amazed everyone.

Meanwhile, a couple named Aquila and Priscilla were quietly listening to Apollos' teachings. Known for their deep love for Jesus and their genuine care for others, they lived out their faith with unwavering devotion. As they listened, they saw the fire in Apollos' eyes and his passion for God's Word. Yet they recognized his understanding of the Gospel was incomplete.

Moved by their love for Christ and their desire to see others know Him fully, Aquila and Priscilla approached Apollos privately. With warm smiles and open hearts, they introduced themselves and explained the way of God to him more accurately.

Apollos had zeal, but he lacked spiritual knowledge. His message was not inaccurate or insincere; it was just incomplete. He spoke and taught *accurately about Jesus, although he knew only John's baptism* (Acts 18:25). He explained Jesus as the Messiah, the one prophesied in Scripture, and appealed for them to repent of their sins. But he knew nothing about Calvary, the resurrection of Christ, or the coming of the Holy Spirit at Pentecost.

Aquila and Priscilla welcomed Apollos with love. They guided him toward a more complete understanding of the Gospel. Their words were filled with compassion as they discussed Jesus' life, death, and resurrection, emphasizing the salvation He provided.

Apollos was a scholar from Alexandria, the leading educational center of the known world. Yet he accepted instruction from people who made their living working with their hands. When Priscilla and Aquila approached him to explain the way of God more accurately, he listened and learned. Their patient instruction opened his eyes to the fullness of God's redemptive plan. From then on, Apollos fearlessly shared the complete Gospel message with anyone who listened.

His humbleness and willingness to learn reminds us that no one has a complete understanding of God's Word. As Christians, God encourages us to remain humble and excited for opportunities to learn and grow in our faith. We can all benefit from the wisdom and insights of others.

Priscilla and Aquila wisely took Apollos aside and did their teaching privately. It would have been unkind of them, as well as humiliating to Apollos, had they attempted to correct him in public. We can all take a lesson from this couple and understand tact is a Christian virtue.

The Apostle Peter wrote to be *ready at any time to give a defense to anyone who asks you for a reason for the hope that is in you.* **Yet do this with gentleness and reverence.** (1 Peter 3:15-16, emphasis mine)

Priscilla and Aquila offer a great example of how to be active in the lives of younger believers, to encourage and teach them with gentleness. They lived the command of Jesus. *Go, therefore, and make disciples of all nations, ... teaching them to observe everything I have commanded you* (Matthew 28:19-20).

They followed the pattern taught by the Apostle Paul. *What you have heard from me in the presence of many witnesses, commit to faithful men who will be able to teach others also* (2 Timothy 2:2). Paul met and taught Aquila and Priscilla, who met and taught Apollos. Apollos then went to Corinth, where he had a successful ministry, leading many to Christ and helping them grow in their faith.

God has entrusted us with the incredible privilege of knowing His Word and experiencing His grace. We are not to keep it to ourselves. When we share the teachings of Christ, we ensure the truth of the Gospel message is preserved and faithfully preached. As we proclaim the Gospel, hearts are changed, lives are healed, and individuals are brought into a loving relationship with Jesus Christ.

The story of Priscilla and Aquila reminds us of the need for discipleship. They guided Apollos in his understanding, and we should actively invest in the spiritual growth of fellow believers. We need to show kindness and patience to those lacking knowledge. Rather than criticizing or condemning, we should gently guide others toward a deeper understanding of God's truth.

95

Priscilla and Aquila are beautiful examples of the Christlike attitudes of love and humility. We can follow their example by sharing God's truth with kindness. By doing so, we reflect the heart of Jesus and support younger believers in their spiritual journey.

Prayer:

Dear Heavenly Father, thank You for the example of Apollos. Like him, may we always be teachable, willing to learn more about You, and have the passion to share Your love with the world. Thank You for Priscilla and Aquila, whose gentle guidance instructed Apollos in a fuller understanding of the Gospel. May Your Spirit inspire within us a desire to train and equip the next generation to carry the torch of faith forward. May we persevere in discipling others until that glorious day when every knee will bow, and every tongue confess that Jesus Christ is Lord. In His name, we pray. Amen.

Action Steps   Date _____

How have you encountered Jesus Christ through today's story?

_____

_____

_____

_____

_____

Based on this story in scripture, what is God calling you to do? In what ways can you demonstrate this?

_____

_____

_____

_____

_____

What are practical ways we can help others develop Christ-like behavior?

_____

_____

_____

_____

_____

Trusting God

Acts 9:10-20

The evening sun cast long shadows over the city of Damascus, but the approaching night paled in comparison to the impending darkness awaiting the believers. The cobblestone streets echoed with nervous whispers of approaching doom. Saul of Tarsus, the notorious persecutor of Christians, was on his way to their beloved city.

The news spread like wildfire. Anxiety and worry filled the disciples' hearts, and fear gripped their souls. All the believers could do was hide behind closed doors and fall to their knees in prayer.

And pray they did. As they prayed, the Lord spoke to Ananias in a vision. He was a kind-hearted man who loved God with all his heart. *"Get up and go to the street called Straight,"* the Lord said to him, *"to the house of Judas, and ask for a man from Tarsus named Saul, since he is praying there* (Acts 9:11).

In his zeal for God, Saul thought he was doing God a favor by eliminating this religious uprising. Instead, he became the church's number one enemy, *breathing threats and murder against the disciples of the Lord* (Acts 9:1).

99

Ananias felt a shiver run down his spine. He knew what Saul had done to the church in Jerusalem and throughout the region. What Ananias was about to discover, however, is what Jesus had done to Saul.

The Lord, in His infinite wisdom, comforted Ananias. God assured him, Saul was now praying instead of persecuting. On the road to Damascus, Saul had seen the light, and was now waiting in darkness, his heart heavy with confusion and repentance.

With a deep breath and unwavering faith, Ananias trusted the Lord's guidance. Knowing God had a plan, he set out for Straight street. With a prayer in his heart, Ananias entered the house where Saul was staying. By the time he arrives, blind Saul began to see Jesus in a different light.

Ananias approached him and said in a gentle, soothing voice, "Brother Saul." How sweet those words must have sounded. He is still Saul of Tarsus, but he is no longer an enemy. Now, he is a brother.

He placed his hands on him and said, "Brother Saul, the Lord Jesus, who appeared to you on the road you were traveling, has sent me so that you may regain your sight and be filled with the Holy Spirit" (Acts 9:17). At that moment, something amazing happened. *At once something like scales fell from his eyes, and he regained his sight* (Acts 9:18). Saul's physical and spiritual blindness were lifted. His eyes, which were once blind, now filled with light, and Saul experienced a transformation in his heart.

Ananias continued to pray for him, and Saul was filled with the Holy Spirit. Within the hour he stepped out of the waters of baptism, and soon he's preaching in the synagogue the first of a lifetime of sermons. Saul eventually becomes known as the Apostle Paul and God used him in a mighty way to touch the world, but first, He used Ananias to touch Paul.

This remarkable encounter between Ananias and Saul provides an inspirational example for us to follow.

Ananias Trusted God

Ananias did not let fear or doubt stop him from obeying God's command. He trusted God's plan and followed His guidance, even when it seemed irrational. Ananias could never have guessed he would be the one to help Saul become a Christian, but he trusted God.

God often works in ways we cannot predict or understand. Sometimes, God may call us to serve in ways that seem unreasonable or uncomfortable. Just as Ananias stepped out in faith despite his reservations, we can be assured God's guidance is always for our ultimate good. We can trust God and walk in faith, knowing He is in control.

Trust in the Lord with all your heart, and do not rely on your own understanding; in all your ways know him, and he will make your paths straight. (Proverbs 3:5-6)

Ananias Willingly Forgave

Ananias demonstrated a remarkable willingness to forgive and extend God's grace to a former enemy of the faith. Rather than look back at what Saul was, Ananias looked forward to what he could become.

Ananias' example encourages us to let go of grudges and prejudices, and show compassion even to those we might find difficult to love. Just as Ananias forgave Saul, we should be open to forgive those who may have wronged us.

> *Be kind and compassionate to one another, forgiving one another, just as God also forgave you in Christ.* (Ephesians 4:32)

Ananias Walked in Obedience

Ananias faced an unexpected opportunity to play a pivotal role in Saul's conversion. Fear could have paralyzed Ananias, preventing him from carrying out God's plan. But Ananias did not just hear God's voice, he obeyed.

Ananias' actions remind us that God uses ordinary people to accomplish extraordinary things when they are obedient to His call. Obedience opens the door for God to work through us in amazing ways. When God calls us to do something, whether big or small, our response should be one of obedience.

> *"Why do you call me 'Lord, Lord,' and don't do the things I say?"* (Luke 6:46)

Ananias became an unsung hero in the early Christian narrative. He was a man whose trust in God and obedience to His will, played a pivotal role in the spread of the Gospel. Like Ananias, each of us has the potential to make a positive impact in the lives of others through our trust and obedience to God.

During His earthly ministry, Jesus said, *"I have come down from heaven, not to do my own will, but the will of him who sent me"* (John 6:38). Jesus trusted and obeyed His Father in everything He did. Nothing He did was outside of God's will. The Apostle Paul wrote of Jesus, *He humbled himself by becoming obedient to the point of death—even to death on a cross* (Philippians 2:8). Ananias was a shining example of the Christlike behavior of trusting and obeying God and a model for us to emulate.

Prayer:

Dear Heavenly Father, we thank You for the story of Ananias and the part he played in the conversion of Saul. Forgive us for the times we may have let fear and prejudice stop us from serving You. Like Ananias, may we reach out in love, forgiving others of their past and share the good news of Your salvation. May his example inspire us to trust You and walk in obedience, knowing that You can use us in remarkable ways for Your glory. In the precious name of our Lord and Savior, Jesus Christ, we pray. Amen.

Action Steps

How have you encountered Jesus Christ through today's story?

_____

_____

_____

_____

_____

Based on this story in scripture, what is God calling you to do? In what ways can you demonstrate this?

_____

_____

_____

_____

_____

What are practical ways we can help others develop Christ-like behavior?

_____

_____

_____

_____

_____

Thank You for Reading
Encountering Christlikeness.

Please join us in ministry in two powerful ways:

First, Pray for Us.

Pray for Christian Growth Ministry as we strive to Encourage Believers to Mature in Their Walk with Christ, Grow in Their Faith, & Serve in Ministry, All for the Glory of God. Pray that God will guide our writing and publishing efforts as we develop additional devotions and resources, and God will use them in a mighty way to uplift Christians around the world and bring Him glory and honor.

Second, Share our Ministry's Work with Others.

Please leave a review for this book on Amazon. Reviews are the single best way for others to learn about these devotions. Tell others how this book has inspired and motivated you to reflect Christ in your life, and deepen your understanding and appreciation of the Bible.

Above all,

Whatever you do, do everything for the glory of God (1 Cor 10: 31).

About the Author

With a unique blend of storytelling and Bible exposition, Brad Simon has shared God's Word for over forty-five years. His passion is to inspire and encourage Christians to grow in their faith and walk closer with the Lord. Brad is the author of the Encounters In Scripture devotional series and is the featured Bible Teacher on Monday Morning Inspiration podcast. He is also a frequent contributor to Refresh Bible Study Magazine and BibleStudyTools.com.

Brad is founder and director of Christian Growth Ministry, working to encourage believers to mature in their walk with Christ, grow in their faith, and serve in ministry, all for the glory of God.

Brad is a retired Master Jeweler. He relies on the God-given creativity that won him several national and international jewelry design awards to craft Biblical Narratives and Life Stories that are engaging and thought-provoking. Once a speaker, author, publisher, and trainer for the jewelry industry, now he is putting those skills to work to promote the beauty and appeal of God's Word.

Originally from Illinois, Brad and his wife Debbie have made Spartanburg, South Carolina, their home for the past twenty-eight years. They are proud parents of two sons (one married) and two grandsons. His one guilty pleasure is being an avid fan of St. Louis Cardinals baseball.

Discover his Bible Teaching Ministry at:
BWSimon.com
Facebook.com/BradSimonTeachingMinistry

Follow Brad Simon on Amazon
Amazon.com/stores/Brad-Simon/author/B0BLGV8MV3

Other titles in the **Encounters In Scripture Devotional Series** include:

Encountering the Master Carpenter
Devotional Portraits of Christ Building the Faith of His Disciples

Encountering Indescribable Peace (booklet)
Free Download at: BWSimon.com/peace

Encounters with God through Prayer (booklet)
Free Download at: BWSimon.com/prayer

Encountering
Indescribable Peace

Get The Ebook

Encounters with God
through Prayer

Get The Ebook

New Titles Coming Soon:

Encountering Christmas
Devotional Portraits of the First Christmas

Encountering Faith in Action
Devotional Portraits of the Church's Foundation

Encountering Pillars of Faith
Devotional Portraits of Hebrews 11

Encountering Voices of Hope
Devotional Portraits of the Minor Prophets

Encountering Church Fathers
Devotional Portraits of Pioneers of the Faith

Monday Morning Inspiration

Join Bible Teacher Brad Simon as Christian Growth Ministry presents Monday Morning Inspiration a Podcast designed to inspire you to grow in the faith and encourage you to walk closer with the Lord. Listen during your drive time or anytime for Inspiration from God's Word.

Listen at: ChristianGrowthMinistry.com
or on your favorite Podcast App.

**Monday Morning
Inspiration**

Listen Here

*Christian
Growth
Ministry*

Working to Encourage Believers to Mature in Their Walk with Christ, Grow in Their Faith, & Serve in Ministry, All for the Glory of God.

ChristianGrowthMinistry.com

Facebook.com/ChristianGrowthMinistries

Refresh Bible Study Magazine

Connecting God's Word to Life Today

*Discover stories, Scripture,
and strategies for the Christian life.*

The mission of Refresh is to connect God's Word to life today. This free, digital magazine published by Lighthouse Bible Studies is sent quarterly to subscribers. Use Refresh for personal encouragement or for small group discussion. Use some of the stories, quotes, or topics as conversation starters to get people talking about God and His Word.

Brad Simon is a frequent contributor to Refresh Magazine. You can receive a free subscription at: LighthouseBibleStudies.com/refresh-bible-study-magazine

Come join us for "Be Refreshed," a weekly discussion of Refresh articles. We meet on Zoom on Thursdays from 7-8 pm eastern time, and hear an author read his or her article, and we discuss it.

To receive the link for the zoom online group E-mail: LighthouseBibleStudies@hotmail.com

Made in the USA
Columbia, SC
12 February 2024

31327452R00072